Sarah's Surprise

Written by
Rob Waring and **Maurice Jamall**

Before You Read

put something in

to call someone

to drink (a drink)

to work

bag

café

cookies

food

husband and wife

ice cream

money

pants and shirt

police officer

sandwich (sandwiches)

surprised

In the story

Sarah

Ji-Sung

Mrs. Hayes

The man

"Hello, Sarah, I'm Mrs. Hayes," says a woman.
"How do you do, Mrs. Hayes?" says Sarah.
Mrs. Hayes has a café. The café's name is The Lagoon.
Sarah starts work at The Lagoon today.

Ji-Sung works at The Lagoon, too.
Mrs. Hayes says to him, "Ji-Sung, this is Sarah. She starts work today."
"Hi Sarah, it's nice to meet you. I'm Ji-Sung," he says.
"Hello, Ji-Sung," says Sarah. "Nice to meet you, too."

			LAGOON'S SALAD	4.00
PITCH BLACK	4.00		CAESAR SALAD	4.50
LAGOON'S BREW	4.25		KING'S SALAD	5.00
COFFEE W/ CREAM	4.50		NEPTUNE'S SALAD	6.50
EXPRESSO	5.00			
COFFEE LATTE	5.50		CAKES	
CAPPUCCINOS			BELGIAN CAKE	3.00
ICED CAPPUCCINO	5.50		CARROT CAKE	3.00
MOCHACCINO	5.50		LEMON CAKE	3.00

ICE CREAM $1.99

Mrs. Hayes shows Sarah the things in the café.
She shows her the drinks and the food.
"This is the coffee maker," she says. "And this is the ice-cream maker."
"Oh, okay," says Sarah.

Ji-Sung and Sarah are working in the café. A man and a woman come into the café.
The woman wants drinks and ice cream.
The man wants some cookies and some sandwiches.

Mrs. Hayes says, "Ji-Sung and Sarah, I'm going out now."
"Okay," says Sarah. "Bye."
Mrs. Hayes goes out.
Sarah and Ji-Sung work in the café.

A man comes into the café. He asks Sarah, "Hello. Is Janet here?"

Sarah says, "Janet? I'm sorry. I don't know Janet."

The man says, "Mrs. Hayes. Where is she?"

Sarah says, "Oh, Mrs. Hayes. She's shopping."

"Okay, thank you," says the man.

The man takes some sandwiches.
He puts them in his bag. He takes an apple, too.
Sarah watches him. She is surprised.
"What's the man doing?" she thinks. "Oh! He's taking the sandwiches."
Ji-Sung does not see the man.

The man does not give the money to Sarah. He says nothing.
He walks out of the café with the food.
Sarah looks at the man. She is very surprised, but she says
nothing.
"What do I do?" she thinks.

"Ji-Sung! Ji-Sung! Come here!" she says.

Ji-Sung comes to Sarah. "Are you okay?" he asks.

Sarah tells Ji-Sung about the man.

"Oh, no," says Ji-Sung.

"What do we do?" Sarah asks.

Ji-Sung says, "Let's call the police."
Sarah calls the police. She tells the police officer about the man.
She says to the police officer, "Yes. Some sandwiches and an apple."
"Okay, thank you," says the police officer. "We are coming now."

A police officer comes to The Lagoon.
Sarah tells the police officer about the man.
"He is a big man," Sarah says. "He has a blue shirt
and white pants. He's about 45 years old."

Mrs. Hayes comes into the café. She sees the police officer. "Hello, Sarah. Why are the police here?" she asks. "Is everything okay?"

Sarah says, "No, Mrs. Hayes. Everything's *not* okay."

She tells Mrs. Hayes about the man.

"Oh, no," says Mrs. Hayes.

Sarah is talking with Mrs. Hayes and the police officer.
She sees the man. He is walking to the café.
"Mrs. Hayes, look! That's the man," says Sarah. "He's coming here!"
Sarah shows them the man. She says, "He has the sandwiches, Mrs. Hayes."

The man sees Mrs. Hayes.

"Is everything okay, Janet?" he asks. "Why are the police here?"

Mrs. Hayes says, "Sarah, this is my husband, Chris. This is *our* café."

She says, "He works near here. He gets his sandwiches here every day."

Sarah is very surprised. "Oh? He's your husband . . . !"